NATIONAL GEOGRAPHIC CHANNEL

GREAT MIGRATIONS

Whales

Laura Marsh

NATIONAL GEOGRAPHIC

Washington, D.C.

For Aunt Linda
—L.F.M.

Paperback ISBN: 978-1-4263-0745-4
Library binding ISBN: 978-1-4263-0746-1

Printed in China
10/RRDS/1

Abbreviation Key: GET = Getty Images; IS = iStockphoto.com; NGS = NationalGeographicStock.com;
NGT = National Geographic Television; SS = Shutterstock.com

Cover, Hiroya Minakuchi/Minden Pictures/NGS; Background water image throughout, Michael Jay/IS; Whale of
a Word throughout: Andrea Danti/SS; 1 (center), Flip Nicklin/Minden Pictures/NGS; 2 (right), Patricio Robles Gil/
Minden Pictures/NGS; 4 (right), Flip Nicklin/Minden Pictures/NGS; 5 (bottom), NGT; 5 (top), John Eastcott & Yva
Momatiuk/NGS; 6 (top), Rob Wilson/SS; 6 (center), Mopic/SS; 6 (bottom), Hugh Lansdown/SS; 7, Peter G. Allinson,
M.D./NGS; 8—9, Peter G. Allinson, M.D./NGS; 10—11, Flip Nicklin/Minden Pictures/NGS; 12 (top center), Flip Nicklin/
Minden Pictures/NGS; 13 (center), Camilla Wisbauer/IS; 14—15 (bottom center), Flip Nicklin/Minden Pictures/NGS;
16—17 (top center), Flip Nicklin/Minden Pictures/NGS; 18—19 (top right), Flip Nicklin/Minden Pictures/NGS; 19
(center), Flip Nicklin/Minden Pictures/NGS; 20—21, Flip Nicklin/Minden Pictures/NGS; 22, Mike Kelly/The Image
Bank/GET; 23 (top), Brigitte Wilms/Minden Pictures/NGS; 23 (center), DJ Mattaar/SS; 23 (bottom), Jason Edwards/
NGS; 25, Flip Nicklin/NGS; 26—27, Flip Nicklin/NGS; 28—29, Hiroya Minakuchi/Minden Pictures/NGS; 30—31
(center), Jason Edwards/NGS; 32 (top left), Hiroya Minakuchi/Minden Pictures/NGS; 32 (bottom right), NGT;
32 (left center), NGT; 32 (right center), Flip Nicklin/Minden Pictures/NGS; 32 (bottom left), Flip Nicklin/Minden
Pictures/NGS; 32 (top right), Flip Nicklin/NGS; 33 (top left), Flip Nicklin/Minden Pictures/NGS; 33 (top right), Hiroya
Minakuchi/Minden Pictures/NGS; 33 (left center), NGT; 33 (bottom), Flip Nicklin/NGS; 33 (bottom right), Flip
Nicklin/Minden Pictures/NGS; 34 (bottom left), Ivanova Inga/SS; 35 (top), Hiroya Minakuchi/Minden Pictures/
NGS; 36 (bottom center), Brian Skerry/NGS; 37 (bottom right), Tyson Mackay/All Canada Photos/GET; 38—39
(top), Hiroya Minakuchi/Minden Pictures/NGS; 38 (bottom), Jiri Rezac/Greenpeace; 40 (left), Igor Stevanovic/SS;
41 (center), Flip Nicklin/Minden Pictures/NGS; 43, Flip Nicklin/Minden Pictures/NGS; 44, Randy Faris/Corbis; 44—45,
Ralph Lee Hopkins/NGS; 46 (top right), Flip Nicklin/Minden Pictures/NGS; 47 (right center), Mogens Trolle/SS; 46
(bottom), Hiroya Minakuchi/NGS; 47 (top left), Patricio Robles Gil/Minden Pictures/NGS; 47 (center right), Peter
G. Allinson, M.D./NGS; 46 (center right), Hiroya Minakuchi/Minden Pictures/NGS; 46 (center left), Flip Nicklin/
Minden Pictures/NGS; 47 (bottom left), Jiri Rezac/Greenpeace; 47 (bottom right), Igor Stevanovic/SS

Table of Contents

On the Move

When animals travel from one region or habitat to another, it is called migration. Animals migrate in search of food or a mate. Migration helps animals survive on Earth.

Many animals migrate. The sperm whale is one of them.

sperm whales

wildebeest

red crabs

Whale of a Word

MIGRATION: Moving from one region or habitat to another for food or a mate

MATE: Either a male or female in a pair. Most animals need a mate to have babies.

What animal . . .

Is longer than a school bus?

Has the largest brain of any animal?

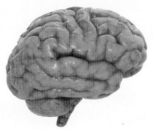

Is one of the greatest divers in the world?

Q Why did the whale cross the road?

A To get to the other tide.

A sperm whale!

Wondrous Whales

Sperm whales are amazing creatures. They are the largest toothed predator on the planet. Males are larger than females. Males weigh up to 50 tons and grow up to 60 feet long. That's not just big, that's H–U–G–E!

How do we measure up?

A sperm whale is so big, it makes an adult human look very small.

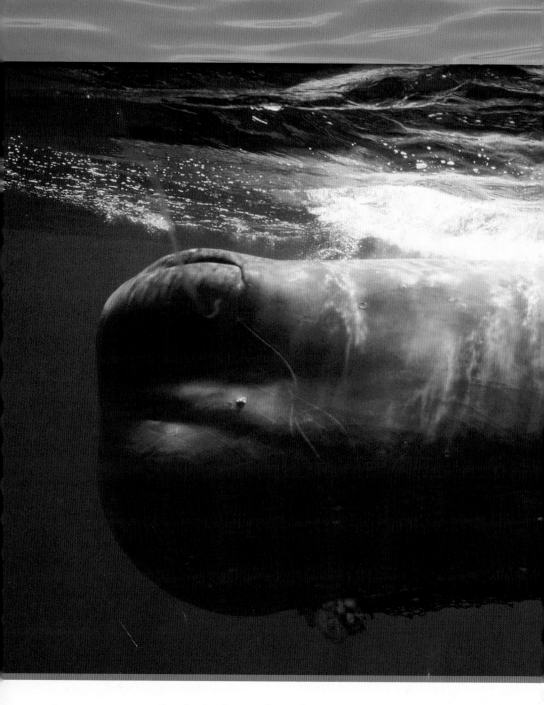

A sperm whale's head is big, too. It makes up one-third of its entire body length.

weird but true

A sperm whale's brain is five and a half times heavier than a human brain.

Its brain is the largest of any animal on Earth and weighs as much as 20 pounds!

Sperm whales get their name from a waxy material in their heads.

Q What do you get when you cross an elephant with a whale?

A A submarine with a built-in snorkel.

Whale Parts in Demand

Spermaceti was once used to make cosmetics, creams, and candles.

It is called spermaceti. You say it like this: spur-mah-SEE-tee. But scientists don't really know what its purpose is.

13

We know a lot about sperm whales.

WEIGHT: 35–50 tons

LENGTH: 49–60 feet

LIFE SPAN: About 70 years

SKIN: Dark gray or black and wrinkled like a prune

TAIL FLUKE: Powers a sperm whale to swim up to 23 miles an hour. The tail fluke is about 16 feet from tip to tip.

weird but true

The heart of the average sperm whale weighs 277 pounds— about as much as two adult humans.

FLIPPERS: Help steer the whale

BLOWHOLE: Used for breathing. Sperm whales can hold their breath for up to 90 minutes.

HEAD: Sperm whales have a massive head and rounded forehead.

BIG TEETH: A sperm whale's lower jaw has 36–50 teeth. Its upper jaw is toothless. Sperm whales are carnivores.

Whale of a Word

CARNIVORE: An animal that only eats meat

Need to Lead

Female sperm whales travel in family groups called pods. There are 15 to 20 females and their young in a pod.

Pods are led by an older female. She guides the whales to the best feeding grounds.

Males usually leave their pods when they are between four and 21 years old. Then they join bachelor groups of up to 50 males. The largest and oldest males tend to swim alone.

Why is being in a pod important?

Sperm whales in a pod stick together as they travel. They protect and care for the sick, young, and injured. They make sure that every whale is fed.

This is important protection since sperm whales migrate very long distances. Some swim enough miles in their lifetimes to circle the Earth several times! They migrate according to the season.

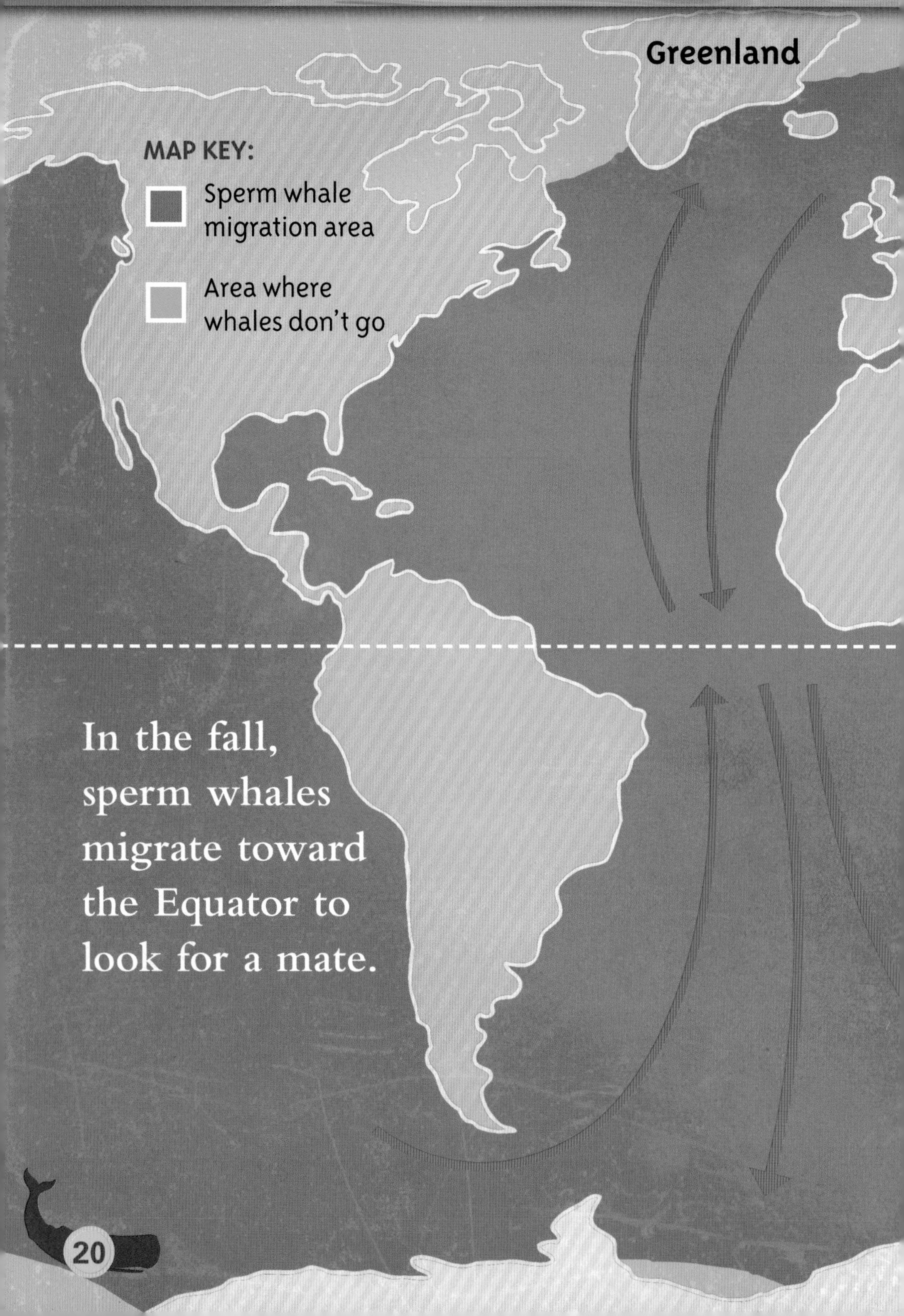

Greenland

In the fall, sperm whales migrate toward the Equator to look for a mate.

20

During the spring and summer, sperm whales swim farther away from the Equator in search of food.

Whale of a Word

EQUATOR: An imaginary line around the Earth, equal distance from the North and South Poles

Female whales and their young stay in the warmer tropical and subtropical waters year round. Males, especially large males, travel much farther. They may swim as far north as Greenland and as far south as Antarctica.

Antarctica

What a Feast!

Sperm whales eat a lot—about one ton of food every day. That's 2,000 pounds! Their favorite food is large squid found in deep waters. They can eat about 700 squid in one day! Sperm whales also eat octopus, fish, shark, and skate.

squid

octopus

fish

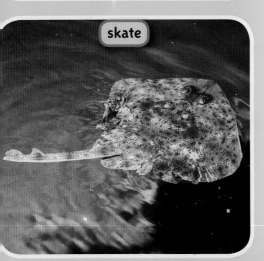

skate

Sometimes there is not enough food in one part of the ocean. While they search for food, whales survive on fat, called blubber, that's stored in their bodies.

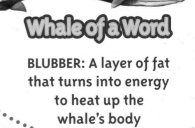

Whale of a Word

BLUBBER: A layer of fat that turns into energy to heat up the whale's body

Deep Sea Divers

Time to dive for dinner!
Sperm whales dive deeper
than any other whale.
They can dive more than
9,000 feet.

How Deep?

How much is 9,000 feet? It's about
1.7 miles. That's the height of about
six Empire State Buildings stacked
on top of each other.

9,000 feet

During an average dive, sperm whales hold their breath for about 45 minutes. They rest on the surface for 10 minutes. Then they dive again. They do this all day long.

Mothers do the hunting for their young. Young whales need to breathe more often than adults. So, they can't dive deep in the ocean until they are older. They wait on the surface and listen for their mothers diving far below them.

Wee Whales

Whales are mammals. Baby whales
are born live and drink their mothers'
milk for the first two years or so of
life. Young whales are called calves.

Calves are born tail first and take their first breath within seconds of being born. They learn to swim within 30 minutes.

Just like human kids, calves can be playful. They play on the surface of the water while older whales are diving.

weird but true

Male sperm whales don't stop growing until they are about 50 years old. Females stop growing at about 30.

10 Cool Things About Sperm Whales

1 Newborns weigh about 1 ton and are 13 feet long.

2 Their heart rate slows during deep dives so they don't waste oxygen.

3 Their teeth are 10 inches long and weigh about 2 pounds each.

4 A sperm whale's blowhole is S-shaped.

5 They smack their tales loudly on the water's surface. It is a mystery why they do this. They might be "talking" to other whales.

6

Many whales in a pod help care for the young.

7

Their eyes are located far back on their heads. They can't see directly in front or in back, only to the side.

8

Some scientists think that spermaceti may help a sperm whale to dive and rise to the surface.

9

Male calves stay with their mothers for at least 4 years. But females stay with their mothers for a lifetime.

10

They are mysterious because they spend most of their time in deep oceans — a place humans can't easily go to study them.

Whale Talk

Sperm whales talk to each other by making clicking sounds. These sounds are also used in echolocation (eh-ko-lo-KAY-shun).

Echolocation is used by animals such as dolphins, bats, and toothed whales to navigate in the dark. Whales send out sound waves that bounce off objects in their path. The sound bounces off the object and returns to the whale. From this they can tell the size and distance of the object.

Whale of a Word

ECHOLOCATION: Using sound waves to locate an object

Whales use echolocation for three purposes:

1 To find their way in the deep, dark ocean,

2 to locate food, and

3 to find their young on the surface of the water.

Deadly Dangers

A giant squid might be a sperm whale's favorite meal—but it's also a whale's worst enemy.

Monstrous Squid!

Giant squid can grow up to 59 feet long and weigh more than one ton. That's as tall as a five-story building and heavier than ten grown men!

Giant squid have the largest eyes of any animal. They are ten inches in diameter.

In fact, some meetings with squid can lead to a deadly fight. Scars shaped like suction cups on a sperm whale's body are signs of a fierce battle with a squid.

Orcas sometimes attack sperm whales, too. When attacked, sperm whales form a circle to protect the sick and young whales. Then they can fight off the attacker with their huge tails.

Greenpeace is an organization that tries
to stop illegal whaling ships, like this
one disguised as a research boat.

During the 1700s, 1800s, and into the 1900s, a large number of whales were killed by people. Sperm whales were hunted for their spermaceti and their oil, which were used to light lamps and make candle wax. Hunters also wanted sperm whales for their ambergris, a material used in perfume.

Kerosene later replaced whale oil as a way to light lamps. Whaling was outlawed in the 1980s. The number of sperm whales has increased. Now there are many sperm whales in our oceans, but illegal whaling still happens.

weird but true

Scientists estimate that whaling has killed one million sperm whales.

Chemicals from factories, boats, and other human activities are dangerous to whales and the environment. This is called pollution. It can make whales sick or even kill them.

Whale of a Word

POLLUTION: Damage to the environment with human-made waste

Whales are also in danger when they get too close to the shore. They can get stuck on beaches in shallow water.

Drawn to Shore

Scientists are not sure why whales sometimes swim toward coastlines. Possible reasons are loud noises, pollution, or unusual weather patterns.

But there is good news.

Organizations are working to stop oil spills and other pollutants in our oceans. People are using fewer plastic bags that may end up in the oceans and hurt sea animals.

Also, researchers are discovering why whales get stranded and what can be done about it.

And there are organizations like Greenpeace working to stop illegal whaling. The Sea Shepherd Conservation Society is another group that enforces whaling laws and saves whales from being killed.

weird but true

The sperm whale's great size allowed it to sometimes sink early whaling ships.